THE FORGIVENESS OF SIN
AS A DEBT

A Sermon Concerning

THE
FORGIVENESS
OF SIN
AS A DEBT

Preached in London, June 1ST, 1711

❧

REV. MATTHEW HENRY
MINISTER OF THE GOSPEL IN CHESTER

CURIOSMITH
MINNEAPOLIS

Published by Curiosmith.
Minneapolis, Minnesota.
Internet: curiosmith.com.

The text of this edition is from *The Miscellaneous Works of the Rev. Matthew Henry*, published by ROBERT CARTER & BROTHERS, 1855.

The "Guide to the Contents" was added to this edition by the publisher.

ISBN 9781946145086

GUIDE TO THE CONTENTS
————o◦⟨◦⊰◦⟩o◦————

THE FORGIVENESS OF SIN AS A DEBT

And forgive us our debts.—Matthew 6:12.
COMPARED WITH
And forgive us our sins.—Luke 11:4.

From this petition in the Lord's prayer, thus differently expressed by the two evangelists, we may easily observe, (for prayer may preach, this prayer preaches,)

I. That sin is a debt to God Almighty; nay, it becomes us to express it with application, (for, so such truths as these look best,) *Our* sins *are our debts.*

II. That the pardon of sin is the *forgiveness of this debt,* and the discharge of the debtor from it: and as the former must be thought of with a penitent application, confessing and bewailing our sins, as our debts, so this with a believing application. This is a privilege offered to us in the gospel: O that we might partake of it!

Repentance and remission of sins, are the two great things which ministers are appointed to preach, in Christ's name, to all nations; and which Christ is himself exalted to the right hand of the Father to give,[1] else our preaching them would be in vain. I am here this day to *preach* them, depending upon divine grace to *give* them; as an ambassador for Christ, to beseech you, by repentance for sin, to be reconciled to God,[2] that by the remission of sin he may be reconciled to you. Brethren, these are matters of life and death, matters of everlasting concern; and therefore challenge your serious attention.

Many of you have a prospect of drawing nigh to the Lord, and having communion with him at his table: and what better service can I do you, than to assist your repentance in your preparations for that ordinance, and to assure you of pardon, upon repentance, in your attendance upon it? To show you sin, that in reflection upon it you may sow in tears; and to show you Christ, that in dependence on him you may reap in joy,[3] and by him may have your tears wiped away.

This similitude, which represents sin as a debt, and the pardon of sin as the forgiving of that debt, our Saviour often used: and it is a proper one, and

1 Luke 24:47; Acts 5:31.
2 2 Corinthians 5:20.
3 Psalm 126:5, 6.

very significant, and I hope by the blessing of God may be of use both to let us into the understanding of this great concern, and to affect us with it.

I. The sins we are to repent of are *our debts to God.*

There is a debt to God, which arises from the command of the law, and we do not pray to be discharged from that: a debt of duty, which we always owe, and must be always paying in the strength of his grace; a yoke so easy, that we cannot desire to be eased of it; a service so reasonable, as that, if we understand ourselves aright, we cannot but be reasoned into it.

We are debtors, not to the flesh,[1] says the apostle; we are under no obligation to serve it and please it, and make provision for it; which intimates that we are debtors *to God:* that which is said to be our *duty to do,*[2] is ὁ ωφειλομεν ποιησαι, that which *we owe the doing of.* We owe adoration to God, as a Being infinitely bright, and blessed, and glorious. We owe allegiance to him as our Sovereign Lord and Ruler. We are bound in honor and duty, in gratitude and interest, to observe his statutes, and to keep his laws; are bound by all the relations we stand in to him as our Creator, Owner, and Benefactor, to love and fear him, and under the influence of those two commanding principles, to serve and obey him: and

1 Romans 8:12.
2 Luke 17:10.

we must reckon it our happiness, that we are thus obliged, and labor to be more and more sensible of the obligations. The loosing of our other bonds strengthens these; so the Psalmist thought, when in consideration thereof he said, *O Lord, truly I am thy servant, I am thy servant,* for thou hast *loosed my bonds.*[1]

There is likewise a debt we owe to one another, which we must not pray to be discharged from, but always kept under the bonds of, and that is, brotherly love. When we are commanded to render to all their due, so as to owe no man any thing; yet we are told we must still owe this, *to love one another;*[2] which when we do we pay a just debt, and yet must still abound more and more.[3]

There is a debt to God, which arises from the curse and condemnation of the law, which we are fallen under, by our breach of the command of the law; and this is that which we here pray to be discharged from: the debt of punishment, that death which we are told is the *wages of sin.*[4] It is a penal bond, by which we are obliged to our duty; so that for nonperformance of the duty we become liable to the penalty: and thus our sins are our debts; and being all sinners, we are all debtors. Know then that

1 Psalm 116:16.

2 Romans 13:8.

3 1 Thessalonians 4:1.

4 Romans 6:23.

the Lord has a controversy[1] with you, an action against you, an action of debt, wherein—in his name—I here arrest you all, pursuant to the great intention of the Spirit, which is to convince the world of sin,[2] to charge men with a debt to God, and to prove it upon them.

In prosecution of this, I shall endeavor to show,

1. How we come to be in debt to God, how this debt is contracted, and what is the ground of the action. That I may keep to the comparison, not forcing it, but fairly following it, you shall see that we run in debt to God, as the children of men run in debt to one another.

(1.) We are in debt to God, *as a servant is indebted to his master*, when he has neglected his business, and wasted or embezzled his goods. Our Saviour represents our case like that of a servant to a king, who when he came to be reckoned with, (probably the revenues of the crown passing through his hands) was found in debt to the king his master *ten thousand talents;*[3] and that of a steward who was *accused to his lord that he had wasted his goods,*[4] either through sloth and negligence, not taking the care and pains about them, that by the duty of his place he ought to have done; or through

---

1 Micah 6:2.
2 John 16:1.
3 Matthew 18:24.
4 Luke 16:1.

dishonesty, converting them to other uses than they were intended for, and serving himself with them.

We are servants to God, and have work to do for the advancing of the interest of his glory and kingdom in the world, and in our own hearts. This work is undone; we have stood all the day idle, and have done nothing, or next to nothing, of the great work we were sent into the world about; nothing to answer the ends of our creation and redemption, and in pursuance of the intentions of our birth and baptism; and so we become to be in debt, and deserve, not only to have our wages stopped, but to lie under the doom of the unprofitable servant, who is therefore called *wicked*, because slothful.[1]

We have been intrusted with talents,[2] which were put into our hands with this charge, *trade till I come;* make use of them in your Master's service, and for his honor: but we have not improved these talents for the end for which we have been intrusted with them, we have hid our Lord's money, have buried our talent, and so we come to be indebted. Time is a talent, it ought to have been filled up with duty; but we have misspent it, and trifled it away, and have not done the work of each day in its day, according as the duty of the day required: we are therefore so much in debt for lost time, time that can never be recalled. Opportunity is a talent, time

1 Matthew 25:26, 30.
2 Luke 19:13.

fitted for the doing of that which will not be done at all, or not so well done another time. The time of youth, sabbath-time, the seasons of grace—the minutes of these are in a particular manner precious; but we have not improved these; we have received the grace of God in them in vain, have had many *a price put into our hands to get wisdom*,[1] which for want of a heart, *a heart at the right hand,* for want of skill, and will, and courage, we have not made the right use of. Our reason is a talent, with all its powers and faculties, which should have been employed in honoring God, but has been so wretchedly misemployed, that *the world by wisdom* (reason doing its best, as it thought) *knew not God.* Our limbs and senses, our bodily health and strength, are talents; for it is designed we should glorify God with our bodies:[2] but the members of our bodies have been instruments of unrighteousness[3] to his dishonor; and for this abuse of them we are indebted. What estate we have in the world, what interest we have in others, or influence upon them, is a talent, puts us in a capacity of serving God, and doing good. But have we done so? No, we have all come short, far short of the glory of God, have come short of glorifying him, and therefore deserve to come short

---

1 Proverbs 17:16.

2 1 Corinthians 6:20.

3 Romans 6:19.

of being glorified with him.[1]

We are stewards of the manifold grace of God:[2] a good stewardship it is, an honorable place, and very profitable. But have we been good stewards? It is *required of stewards that they be faithful;*[3] but when instead of living to God, and doing all to his glory, we live to ourselves,[4] eat and drink to ourselves, when self in every thing must be gratified, and self glorified, and our own things sought more than the things of Christ,[5] then, like unfaithful stewards, we convert that to our own use which should have been laid out for our Masters honor; and upon this account we are in debt.

(2.) We are indebted to God, *as a tenant is indebted to his landlord,* when he is behind of his rent, or has committed waste upon the premises. We are all tenants to God Almighty, tenants at will; all things we have, pertaining both to life and godliness, which contribute to the welfare both of body and soul, we hold by, from, and under him; ever since we came into the world we have breathed in his air, gone upon his ground, and lived upon the gifts of his providence; nay, we have not only been, as creatures, his tenants on the common,

---

1 Romans 3:23.

2 1 Peter 4:10.

3 1 Corinthians 4:2.

4 Zechariah 7:6.

5 Philippians 2:21.

poor cottagers, but, as Christians, he has let out his vineyard to us, as to husbandmen, that he might receive the fruits of it,[1] and that we also might share in its products, and might have the comfort of it, which we gave him the glory of. If Solomon have a thousand pieces of silver from his vineyard at Baal-hamon, they who keep the fruit thereof shall have two hundred.[2]

We have no reason then to complain of a hard bargain; we are not tied to a rack-rent, it is only a chief; it is only a part of the fruits of the vineyard itself; yet this rent has been unpaid, or not paid in current coin. Our love to him (that is the rent demanded) has been cold, it is well if it have not been counterfeit. It is required, that as tenants we do homage to our Lord; (*I become your man*, that is the form) but we have not done it, or not done it from the heart, which he looks at, and requires; but (as among men) it degenerates into a mere formality. There are services to be performed, neither hard nor dishonorable; for what greater honor can we do ourselves than to honor him? and yet those services have been neglected, and left undone. God has come to his vineyard *looking for grapes*, but *behold wild grapes*.[3] Upon these accounts we are indebted, and are liable to be distrained upon, and

---

1 Matthew 21:33, 34.
2 Song of Solomon 8:11, 12.
3 Isaiah 5:2.

all we have seized. Our lives and beings, and all our comforts, are forfeited into the hands of divine justice; and, if we had not had a very patient landlord, the forfeiture had been taken long ago, and we had been broke, and for ever ruined.

When Belshazzar, the greatest monarch upon earth in his time, is (if I may so say) served with an ejectment by the prophet Daniel, in God's name; and, for arrears of rent to the King of Kings, has a vast and rich kingdom subjected to an extent, by the mystic characters, *Mene, Mene*—it is *numbered and finished*, it is thine no more, but it is to be put into other hands; (and yet even this comes short of making good the arrears, for still he is *Tekel— weighed in the balances, and found deficient,*[1] insolvent) one would think surely the debt was very extraordinary: and yet that which the declaration upon this ejectment charges him with, is the same that we are every one of us chargeable with: *The God in whose hand thy breath is, and whose are all thy ways, hast thou not glorified;*[2] thou hast not rendered to God the things that are his, nor paid thy rent, and therefore art turned out.

Our own souls are the vineyards which are let out to us; we are made keepers of these vineyards, are obliged to keep them in good repair, and by constant watchfulness to keep up the fences about

1 Daniel 5:26, 27.
2 Daniel 5:23.

them; but we have neglected them, and they have been like *the field of the slothful, and the vineyard of the man void of understanding, all grown over with thorns*, the fruits of the curse, and the stone wall thereof broken down.[1] All our enjoyments we receive from God, and they also have been wasted and misemployed. That has been made the food and fuel of our lusts, which should have been oil to the wheels of our obedience. Thus we have forfeited our own souls, and deserve to be put out of the possession and enjoyment of them: *This night shall thy soul be required.*[2] What shouldst thou do with a soul, who knowest no better what to do with it? Thus all our enjoyments are forfeited. When Israel prepared for *Baal* the corn, and wine, and oil which *God* gave them, he justly threatens to return and take it from them, and to "recover it":[3] it is a law term: he will recover it, as the lord in an action of waste recovers *locum vastatum—waste land;* for when God judges, he will overcome.

(3.) We are indebted to God, *as a borrower is indebted to the lender.* God has bestowed many mercies upon us, has been loading us with his benefits all our days; that is, he has been lending to us according as the case has required. Our natures are necessitous, and continually depending upon the

---

1 Proverbs 24:30, 31.

2 Luke 12:20.

3 Hosea 2:8, 9.

divine providence: the new nature is always craving from the divine grace. God has lent us health, estate, relations, and comfort in them. He has lent us the means of grace, Bibles, ministers, sacraments, and the consolations of his Spirit. He has never been to us as a wilderness, or a land of darkness, or as waters that fail.

But what have we rendered to the Lord for all his benefits toward us?[1] What grateful acknowledgments have we made for his favors to us? Alas! we have all reason to reproach ourselves for that which Hezekiah is charged with, that we have not rendered again according to the benefit done unto us.[2] And thus we come to be in debt. God has sown plentifully upon us, and yet hath reaped sparingly from us; has *given us richly all things to enjoy*,[3] and yet we have served him very poorly. The series of God's mercies has been constant, but the course of our duties has been interrupted, and frequently broken off. When we reflect upon the goodness and mercy which has followed us all the days of our life, and come to ask, *What honor and what dignity hath been done*[4] to our great Benefactor for all this; we find our returns of duty and thankfulness no way answerable to our receivings of mercy, and so we become to be in debt.

---

1 Psalm 116:12.
2 2 Chronicles 32:25.
3 1 Timothy 6:17.
4 Ester 6:3.

This debt is still the greater, in that we have made not only poor returns, but ill returns, to the God of our mercies: he has nourished and brought us up as children, and yet we have rebelled against him;[1] he has loaded us with benefits, and yet we have loaded him with our iniquities: thus have we requited the Lord, like foolish people and unwise.[2] Much of our debt is contracted by the most base ingratitude imaginable to the best of friends, the best of fathers; and if you call a man *ungrateful*, you can call him *no worse*.

(4.) Our debt to God is, *as the debt of a trespasser to him upon whom he has trespassed*. Our sins, which are here in the Lord's prayer called, *our debts,* in the verses following are called παραπτωματα— our trespasses,[3] and thence we commonly use that word, in repeating the Lord's prayer. An action of damage differs not much from an action of debt, and this action lies against us as sinners.

We have broken through the fences and bounds which God by his commands has set us, and by which our appetites and passions should have been restrained and kept within compass; and so we are trespassers in debt to God, for trampling his law under foot, and his authority, as if we were resolved to be like our forefathers at Babel, from whom

1 Isaiah 1:3.
2 Deuteronomy 32:6.
3 Matthew 6:15.

nothing would be restrained that they imagined to do.[1]

Nay, we have broken in upon God's rights, have invaded his prerogatives, by taking that praise to ourselves which is due to him only. We have gone upon forbidden ground, and like our first parents have eaten the fruit of the forbidden tree, by enriching ourselves with unlawful gains, and indulging ourselves in unlawful pleasures, meddling with that of which the Lord our God has said, *Ye shall not eat of it,*[2] *neither shall ye touch it.* By presuming on comforts which we were not entitled to, we become trespassers; as he was that intruded into the wedding-feast, not having on a wedding-garment: *Friend, how camest thou hither?*[3]

By those trespasses upon the divine authority, we have injured God, have injured him in his honor. (And the creature cannot otherwise be injurious to the Creator but in his honor; *If thou sinnest, what dost thou against him?*)[4] By this, we are indebted to him; satisfaction is demanded for the injury: for *Shall a man rob God,*[5] and never be called to an account for it? trespass upon him, impeach his honor, and invade his property, and never hear of it?

---

1 Genesis 11:6.
2 Genesis 2:7.
3 Matthew 22:12.
4 Job 35:6.
5 Malachi 3:8.

(5.) Our debt to God is *as the debt of a covenant breaker*, who entered into articles, and gave bond for performance, but has not made good his agreement, and so has forfeited the penalty of the bond, which is recoverable as far as the damage goes, by the non-performance of the articles. An oath is called a "Bond upon the soul," because it was commonly made with an imprecation of evil, if the promise was not performed; so that he who broke his promise so ratified, could not but feel himself under the burden of his own curse.

This is our case; we are bound out from all sin, and bound up to all duty, not only by the bond of a command, but by the bond of a covenant, to which we have ourselves subscribed with the hand; we have by solemn promise engaged ourselves to be the Lord's, to walk in his ways, and to keep his statutes;[1] our baptism was an early and lasting obligation upon us to be religious: but we have broken our covenant with God, have violated our engagements, and thereby have not only forfeited the blessings of the covenant, but made ourselves obnoxious to the curses of it; and so we are in debt to God, as they were who transgressed the covenant which they made before God when they cut the calf in twain,[2] wishing that they might so be cut asunder, if they did not deal faithfully. This is assigned as the ground

1 Deuteronomy 26:17.
2 Jeremiah 34:18.

of God's controversy with the world of mankind, and for which they are all laid under the arrest of his curse; they have *changed the ordinance*, and *broken the everlasting covenant, therefore hath the curse devoured the earth.*[1]

(6.) Our debt to God is *as the debt of a malefactor, to the law and to the government*, when he is found guilty of treason or felony, and consequently the law is to have its course against him. And this is the most proper notion of the debt of sin; for though our Saviour in his parables alludes to money-debts, yet the case between God and man is not as that between debtor and creditor in commerce: for God is our Sovereign, and we are his subjects; he is our Law-giver, and we are bound by his laws. The primary obligation is the command of the law, to obey that; which if we fail in, we fall under a secondary obligation to the curse of the law; and therefore as many as being sinners are under the law, are under the curse, for so it is written, *Cursed is every one, that continues not in every thing that is written in the book of the law to do it.*[2] But God knows, and our own hearts know, that we have not continued, no not in any thing; we are all guilty before God,[3] subject to his judgment. The Scripture hath *concluded us all under sin;* shuts us up as debtors and

---

1 Isaiah 24:5, 6.
2 Galatians 3:10.
3 Romans 3:19.

criminals are shut up in prison, that the law may have its course.

We have all broken the commands of the law, and so are become liable to the sentence of it, *The soul that sins shall die*,[1] shall die, as a soul can die; shall be made completely miserable. Our blessedness is forfeited, as the life, honor, and estate of a traitor is to the public justice, to which he is thus to make the uttermost satisfaction he is capable of making: the case is ours, and a deplorable case it is. As the corruption of our nature makes us odious to God's holiness, so our many actual transgressions make us obnoxious to his justice; and thus we are debtors to him.

(7.) To make the matter yet worse, there is a debt we owe to God, which is *as a debt of an heir-at-law upon his ancestor's account*, of a son who is liable to his father's debts, as far as what he has by descent will go, and as far as he has any assets in his hand. By Adam's disobedience we were all made sinners,[2] we were all made debtors; and laid under this charge, *That we are a seed of evil doers.*

The human nature comes to us as by descent from our first parents, and it comes to us not only distempered but attainted by law; as the blood of a traitor is corrupted by his attainder. When those are under the dominion of death who yet never sinned

1 Ezra 18:4.
2 Romans 5:19.

after the similitude of Adam's transgression,[1] and God visits the iniquity of the fathers upon the children, we must own ourselves indebted on the score of those who are gone before us.

(8.) There are debts of ours, likewise, which are *as the debt of a surety upon account of the principal*. I mean the guilt we have contracted by our partaking of other men's sins,[2] and making ourselves accessary to them, as if we had not had guilt enough of our own to answer for.

We have, by the influence of our example, by advice or encouragement, by contributing to their temptations, or exciting their corruptions, or by a consent and approbation *ex post facto—after the deed has been done*, made ourselves partners with others in sin, and have had *fellowship with the unfruitful works of darkness*, which we should rather have reproved; and so must answer not only for our doings, but for the fruit of our doings.

Having opened up to you the several ways how we come into this debt to God, let as next inquire what kind of debt sin is.

(1.) It is an *old debt*, it is an early, nay, it is an hereditary, encumbrance upon our nature. The foundation of this debt was laid in Adam's sin, we are in debt for the forbidden fruit he ate, so high does the account begin, and so far back does it

---

1 Romans 5:14.
2 1 Timothy 5:22.

look. We were born in debt, were *called*, and not miscalled, *Transgressors from the womb*,[1] debtors from the womb; we began betimes to go astray from God, and so to run farther and farther into debt: it has been long in the contracting, and continual additions have been made to it, by renewed acts of rebellion against God. Job when he is old is made to *posses the iniquities of his youth*,[2] and Ephraim *bears the reproach of his youth*.[3] And how earnestly does David pray, *O remember not the sins of youth.*[4]

(2.) It is *just debt*, and the demand of it highly equitable. We cannot say that we are charged with more than is meet;[5] no, how high soever the penalty is with which we are loaded, certainly it is less than our iniquities have deserved.[6] It is divine justice, the eternal rule and fountain of justice, that charges us with this debt, and brings this action against us; and we are sure that the judgment of God is according to truth; nor is he unrighteous who takes vengeance.[7]

(3.) It is a *great debt*, more than we imagine. It is represented by our Savior as a debt of ten thousand talents.[8] In the computation of money, a talent

---

1 Isaiah 48:8.
2 Job 13:26.
3 Jeremiah 31:19.
4 Psalm 25:7.
5 Job 34:23.
6 Job 11:6.
7 Romans 2:2, 3, 5.
8 Matthew 18:24.

is the highest denomination, it amounts to above 187 pounds of our money; multiply that by ten thousand, and what an immense sum does it come to. This is designed to show us what a great deal of malignity there is in every sin, how heinous it is in its own nature, it runs as a *talent* in debt; and withal how numerous our sins are, how many, how very many, our actual transgressions, they are *ten thousands*, more than the hairs on our heads. Well might the master say to that servant, when he upbraided him with his pardon, *I forgave thee that great debt.*

(4.) It is *a growing debt;* a debt we are still adding to, as a tenant who is behind of his rent, every rent-stage makes the rent more: till we return by repentance, we are still running further upon the score; still taking up upon trust, and treasuring up onto ourselves guilt and wrath against the day of wrath.[1]

3. Having seen what kind of debt sin is, let us next see what kind of debtors sinners commonly are; and we shall find them like other unfortunate debtors, that are going down in the world, and have no way to help themselves.

(1.) Bad debtors are oftentimes very *careless* and unconcerned about their debts; when they are so embarrassed and plunged that they cannot *bear* the thought of it, they contrive how to *banish* the thought of it, and live merry and secure; to laugh away, and drink away, and revel away the care and

1 Romans 2:5.

sorrow of it. Thus sinners deal with their convictions, they divert them with the business of the world, or drown them in the pleasures of sense. Cain endeavored to shake off the terrors of conscience, by building a city.[1] It was once said of one who died over head and ears in debt, "Surely his pillow had some extraordinary virtue in it to dispose a man to rest, else one in that condition could not repose himself upon it." One would wonder what pillows sinners lay their heads on, who have been so *long* in debt, who are so *deep* in debt to the justice of God, and never lay it to heart, nor inquire into the things which belong to their peace. O what multitudes of precious souls are lost, and perish for ever, through mere carelessness!

(2.) Bad debtors are commonly very *wasteful*, and when they find they are in debt more than they can pay, care not how much further they run into debt. How extravagant are sinners in spending upon their lusts! What waste do they make of their time and opportunity, and of the noble powers and faculties with which they are endued! like the prodigal son, who, when he was run away from his father's house info a far country, there wasted his substance with riotous living. So true is that of Solomon, *One sinner destroys much good,*[2] with which he might honor God, and do service to his generation; and

---

1 Genesis 4:17.
2 Ecclesiastes 9:18.

runs through a great deal of valuable treasure.

(3.) Bad debtors are commonly very *shy of their creditors*, and very loth to come to an account. Thus sinners care not how little they come into the presence of God, but rather say to the Almighty, *Depart from us;* they take no pleasure in hearing from him, in speaking to him, or in having any thing to do with him; they desire not the knowledge of his good ways, lest thereby they should come to the sight of their own evil ways. They are shy of communion with their own hearts, and looking into their consciences, because they are not willing to know the worst by themselves. God hearkens and hears, but they speak not aright;[1] they do not take the first step toward repentance and conversion, for they make no serious reflections upon themselves, they never ask, *What have I done?* But the case of those tradesmen is justly suspected, who are strangers to their books, and are afraid of knowing what posture their affairs are in.

(4.) Bad debtors are sometimes *timorous;* and though they strive to cast off all care about their debts, yet, when they are threatened, their hearts fail them, they are subject to frights, and are ready to think every one they meet is a bailiff. Thus sinners carry about with them a misgiving conscience, which often reproaches them, and fills them with secret terrors, and a bitterness which their own

1 Jeremiah 8:6.

heart only knows. When Cain was under an arrest for that great debt he contracted by the murder of his brother, what a terror was he to himself, crying out, *My punishment is greater than I can bear,*[1] though it was much less than he deserved. When Herod heard of Christ's miracles, he presently cried out, *It is John the Baptist whom I beheaded*, he is certainly risen from the dead. The wicked are sometimes made to flee where no fear is, much more where there is fear.

(5.) Bad debtors are apt to be *dilatory* and *deceitful*, to promise payment this time and the other, but still to break their word, and beg a further delay. It is so with sinners; they do not say they will never repent, and return to God, but not yet: *The time is not come, the time that the Lord's house should be built,*[2] but they will assure you, that some time or other it shall be built. They are called to come to an account with their own consciences, to search and try their ways; and they are forward to promise that they will do it; nay, they will set the time when they will do it. The servant that owed ten thousand talents thought he needed not be beholden to his master for a pardon of the debt, only he begged forbearance: *Have patience with me and I will pay thee all.*[3] They shake off their convictions, and

---

1 Genesis 4:13.
2 Haggai 1:2.
3 Matthew 18:29.

elude them, by shifting off the prosecution of them, like Felix, to a more convenient season, which season never comes; and so they are cozened of all their time, by being cozened of the present time.

4. To affect you the more with the misery of an impenitent, unpardoned state, having showed you what your debt is, I shall next lay before you the danger we are in by reason of this debt. Many who owe a great deal of money, yet are furnished with considerations sufficient to make them easy, but they are such as our case will not admit.

(1.) *An exact account is kept of all our debts.* Some who are in debt please themselves with hopes that their debts cannot be proved upon them, and so they shall escape harm by them: but this will do us no service; all our sins will be proved upon us. *These things thou hast done:*[1] it is in vain to deny it, or to avoid the action by pleading *Non est factum—It is not thy deed.* If the debtor keep not an account of his debts, yet the creditor does; they are all booked, all kept on record, laid up in store with God, and sealed among his treasures.[2] Job speaks of his transgressions as sewed up in a bag,[3] as the indictments are upon which the prisoners are to be arraigned; or, as bonds and notes are carefully tied up together to be produced when there is occasion.

---

1 Psalm 50:21.
2 Deuteronomy 32:34.
3 Job 4:17.

It will be to no purpose to contest the account, when the omniscience of God will attest it. *Went not my heart with thee?*[1] says the prophet to his servant. Was not God's eye upon us, when our backs were upon him, and we were running from him into bypaths? Were not all our ways, our sinful ways, ever before him? They were, without doubt they were; but therefore sinners are secure, and see not their danger, because (says God) *they consider not in their heart that I remember all their wickedness.*[2] But consider this, ye who forget God,[3] and his goodness, that God does not forget you and your wickedness. Our sins are never *cast behind his back*, till we have set them *before our faces*.

(2.) *We are utterly insolvent, and have not wherewithal to pay our debts.* If a man be much in debt, yet if he knows he has wherewithal to answer all his creditors, he needs not much perplex himself, especially, if he can discount with his creditors themselves: and there are those who flatter themselves with a conceit, that this will help them in their dealing with God. For being ignorant of his righteousness, of the strictness of the demands of his justice, they go about to establish a righteousness[4] of their own, and are willing to hope that

---

1 2 Kings 5:26.
2 Hosea 7:2.
3 Psalm 50:22.
4 Romans 10:3.

their good qualities, and their good deeds, will atone for their bad ones, and be a competent satisfaction to the demands of divine justice. Thus it is common for foolish debtors to talk big, as if they had wherewithal to give every body their own, and nobody should lose by them, when, perhaps, their all is nothing, or next to nothing. Laodicea thought herself rich and increased in goods, when she was wretchedly and miserably poor and naked,[1] but withal blind, and would not see.

But what good will it do us thus to deceive ourselves? Can the all-seeing God be deceived? It is certain we owe more than we are worth; whether our debt be more or less, five hundred pence, or fifty, we are not able to pay it.[2] We cannot plead that we have, by any services to God, or sufferings for him, made satisfaction for any part of our debts; nor can we promise that we will; for whatever good there is in us, it is God's own gift, it is his own work, for which we are yet more indebted to him. Whatever good is done by us, it is what we are already bound to. And though a tenant should pay his rent for the future, yet that will not discharge his old scores. We are become bankrupts, must own ourselves so, and for ever undone, if the debt we owe be exacted; for if God enter into judgment with us, and deal with us in strict justice according to our deserts, we are

1 Revelation 3:17.
2 Luke 7:41, 42.

not able to answer him for one of a thousand.[1] *In thy sight,* Lord, *shall no flesh living be justified.* We have no oil to sell, as the prophet's widow had, wherewith to pay our debt; no equivalent to offer, nor any thing wherewith to make a composition. We are debtors to God, but he is no debtor to us, nor is he ever behind-hand with those who do any service for him: none has first given to him, that it should be recompensed to him again.[2] There were those indeed who thought they had made God their debtor by their devotions. *Wherefore have we fasted, say they, and thou seest not?*[3] But when the matter comes to be looked into, it appears that they are debtors to God, by reason of the wickedness of their conversations: *Ye fast for strife and debate.*

(3.) We have no friend on earth who can or will pass his word for us, or be our bail. Many poor debtors encourage themselves with this, that they have some kind relations, who will stand by them, and appear for them, and help them in a time of need: but poor sinful men can have no such prospect, since all their kindred are in the same helpless condition with themselves, as deep in debt as they are. The wealthiest worldlings, who have most money, cannot with it undertake to pay our debts to God: no, *we are not redeemed with corruptible*

---

1 Job 9:3.
2 Romans 11:35.
3 Isaiah 58:3, 4.

things, as silver and gold.[1] Pardons are those gifts of God, which are not to be purchased with money in the court of heaven;[2] those, therefore, that are so purchased in the court of Rome, are but sham pardons; even those who boast themselves in the multitude of their riches, yet none of them can by any means redeem his brother.[3] The wisest virgins, who have most grace, have most oil, yet have none to spare, there is not enough for us and them. If God contend with us, no man on earth, or angels in heaven, can undertake to arbitrate the matter, or as a *Days-man, lay his hand upon us both;*[4] can undertake to open the book by which we stand charged, or to loose the seals; none can do it but *the Lion of the tribe of Judah.*[5]

(4.) We are often put in mind of our debts by the providence of God, and by our own consciences. Some who are in debt hope to have benefit by the statute of limitations, and that the debt will be dropped for want of being demanded; but the debts we owe to God are ever and anon demanded, and the right is kept up by a continual claim. God makes it to appear that he takes notice of them, for he frequently gives us notice of them.

1 1 Peter 1:18.
2 Acts 8:20.
3 Psalm 49:6, 7.
4 Job 9:33.
5 Revelation 5:5.

Conscience is a standing monitor in our own bosoms, to put us in mind of our sins, and of the danger we are in by reason of them, and to stir us up to think of agreeing with our adversary in time. For this reason, they who resolve to go on in sin, and to have peace (such as it is) though they go on, do all they can to stifle the suggestions of their own consciences, and turn a deaf ear to them; as those who are in debt avoid them by whom they are dunned, and keep out of their way. But sooner or later conscience will be heard, and will force sinners to say, as Joseph's brethren did long after they had contracted the debt, *We are verily guilty concerning our brother.*[1]

Afflictions are messengers sent to us on this errand, to remind us of our debts, by awaking our consciences, and setting our sins in order before us: when bitter things were written against us, it is with this design, to make us possess our iniquities.[2] When God distrains upon our comforts, and removes them from us, it is to remind us of the arrears of our rent. *Art thou come to call my sin to my remembrance,*[3] (said the widow of Sarepta) *and to slay my son?* These sharp methods, which God takes to put us in mind of our sins, are intimations how severe the reckoning will be, if we never take

1 Genesis 41:21.
2 Job 13:26.
3 1 Kings 17:18.

care to get them pardoned.

(5.) *Death will shortly arrest us for these debts*, to bring us to an account. It is a sergeant, whose office is to require the soul, to strip it of the body, and to bring it to him who gave it, and to whom it is accountable. The authority of this officer is not to be disputed, nor his power resisted. When we are summoned by death to come to an account, we shall find there is no discharge in that war,[1] no remedy, but we must yield. *The wages of sin is death*,[2] and its constant attendant ever since it first entered.[3] Death is our discharge from other debts; in the grave the prisoners rest together, and hear not the voice of the oppressor,[4] but it lays us more open than ever to these debts, for *"After death the judgment."* It is a maxim in our law, *Actio moritur cum personâ—The action dies with the person;* but it will be of no use to us in this case, for God, the creditor, never dies, and sinners, the debtors, are by death fetched in to appear before him.

(6.) *A day of reckoning will come*, and the day is fixed. As sure as we see *this* day, we shall see *that* day, when every man must give an account of himself unto God,[5] *and every work shall be brought*

---

1 Ecclesiastes 8:8.

2 Romans 6:23.

3 Romans 5:12.

4 Job 3:18.

5 Romans 14:12.

into judgment, with every secret thing.[1] The young man who indulges himself in carnal mirth and sensual pleasures, is told that *for all these things God shall bring him into judgment.*[2] Though it is after a long time, yet it is in the set time, that the Lord of the servants, to whom the talents were committed, comes and reckons with them.[3] The God to whom we stand indebted, is one with whom we now have to do;[4] for we live upon him, and subsist by him, and have continual business with him, which should make it the more uneasy to us to think of lying under his displeasure. But that is not all, he is one προς ὸν ἡμιν ὁ λογος (as some read those words)—*to whom for us there is a reckoning;* we now have an account *with* him, and must shortly give up our account *to* him. How careful should we be so to judge ourselves, that we may not be judged of the Lord;[5] so to state our accounts, and balance them with the blood of Christ, that when the day of reckoning comes, we may give up our account with joy, and not with grief![6]

(7.) *Hell is the prison* into which those debtors will at length be cast, who took no care to make

---

1 Ecclesiastes 12:14.
2 Ecclesiastes 11:9.
3 Matthew 25:19.
4 Hebrews 4:31.
5 1 Corinthians 11:31.
6 Hebrews 13:17.

their peace, and there are the tormentors to which they will be delivered.[1] This our Saviour gives as a reason why we should agree with our adversary quickly, while we are in the way, because, if the matter be left to run on, we shall be delivered to the judge, to the officer,[2] to him who has the power of death; and so be cast into prison, into *chains of darkness*, a prison, the miseries of which are *endless* and *easeless*. It is a pit in which there is no water, not the least mixture or allay of comfort, not a drop of water, so much as to cool the tongue.[3] Some prisoners for debt live so merrily, that one would think their prisons were designed for their protection rather than their punishment; but hell is no such prison; there is nothing there but *weeping, and wailing, and gnashing of teeth*, and the more for the many fair warnings given those prisoners not to come into that place of torment. It is a pit out of which there is no redemption; the debtor shall not depart thence till he has paid the last mite; which will never be, no, not during the endless ages of eternity.

And now, sirs, what say you to these things? You are many of you great dealers in the world; what a consternation would you be in, if upon casting up your books, you should discover yourselves to be in

1 Matthew 18:34.

2 Matthew 5:25.

3 Luke 16:24.

debt a great deal more than you are worth? You see you are so to God, and does it make no impression upon you? are you in no care, no concern about it? Is all I have said to you for your conviction of sin, and of your misery and danger because of sin, but as a tale that is told? If so, all I have to say concerning the pardon of sin, will be but *as a lovely song of one that can play well on an instrument.* But I trust you have laid, and will lay, these things to heart, that the debt of sin is really a burden to you, under which you labor, and are heavy laden; and if so, the doctrine of the remission of sins will be to you *glad tidings of great joy*, and as *life from the dead.* Nor would I have taken this pains to show you your sins, if your case had been desperate, and I could not at the same time have showed you the great salvation from sin, which the Redeemer has wrought out by bringing in an everlasting righteousness.

II. The sins we are to repent of, being our debts to God, *the mercy we are to pray for is the forgiveness of these debts.* It is to God we are indebted, and therefore to him we must address ourselves for a discharge from the debt; for none can forgive sins, but God only, and therefore to him only must we go for that forgiveness. Having opened the wound, and showed you how dangerous it is, you will be ready to ask, *Is there no balm in Gilead? Is there no physician there?* Yes, blessed be God, there is. The same messengers that God sends to put you in mind of your debts, are appointed to put you in the way of obtaining the remission of them: and this is that which, in Christ's name, is preached to all nations—it is now preached to you.

1. Let us inquire, *what is included in this mercy* of the forgiveness of sin as a debt, and what steps God graciously takes therein toward us, when we repent, and return, and believe the gospel. He acts as a merciful and compassionate creditor toward a poor debtor who lies at his mercy.

(1.) He stays process, and suffers not the law to have its course. Judgment is given against us; but execution is not taken out upon the judgment. The sinner is arrested by his own conscience as a debtor, and cried out against himself, *I have sinned*, and deserve to die. But pardoning mercy unties the knot between sin and death, and says, as Nathan to David, *The Lord has taken away thy sin, thou shalt not die;*[1] thou shalt not come into condemnation, thine iniquity is become thy grief and shame, and therefore fear not, it shall not be thy ruin. Thou shalt not have all thou hast seized on, thou shalt not go to prison, as thou deservest. The debt shall not be laid to thy charge.

The sinner is arrested by affliction, it may be, as Elihu's penitent is, and is alarmed by it to expect a much sorer punishment; *He is chastened with pain upon his bed, and the multitude of his bones with*

1 2 Samuel 12:13.

strong pain;[1] and then, under the sense of guilt and dread of wrath, counts upon nothing else but that his life shall go to the destroyers.[2] But he has a friend with *him, an interpreter, one among a thousand,*[3] who shows him God's uprightness; his hatred of sin; and yet his readiness to pardon sinners. This he begins to give heed to, and take hold of, and thinks of returning to God, as the prodigal to his father's house; and then *he is gracious to him;*[4] meets him in his return, and says. *Deliver him from going down to the pit;* let him be discharged from these pains, from these terrors, for *I have found a ransom*, a ransom for the soul. The sinner has said unto God, *Do not condemn me;*[5] and God has said, *There is no condemnation to them that are in Christ Jesus.*[6] They in their repentings condemn themselves; men in their reproaches condemn them; and it cannot be denied, but that there is that in them which deserves condemnation. But *it is God that justifies,* and then *who is he that shall condemn?* Christ died, and therefore the believer shall not: he is afflicted and chastened of the Lord, but he shall not be condemned with the world,[7] that lies under the curse.

1 Job 33:19.
2 Job 33:22.
3 Job 33:23.
4 Job 33:34.
5 Job 10:2.
6 Romans 8:1.
7 1 Corinthians 11:32.

Well, this is a good step toward the forgiving of the debt; now there begins to be hope in Israel concerning this thing; herein appears the divine pity and compassion, God's slowness to anger, and readiness to show mercy; and this long-suffering of the Lord is salvation.[1] But the proceedings may perhaps be stopped for the present, and yet may be revived another time; a judgment that has long lain dormant may come against a man when he least thinks of it, and therefore God in forgiving these debts goes further; for,

(2.) He *cancels the bond*, vacates the judgment, and disannuls the hand-writing that was against us, that was contrary to us, and takes it out of the way.[2] He pardons sin thoroughly and fully, so as to remember it no more[3] against the sinner. He casts it behind his back,[4] as that which he is determined never more to inquire after; casts it into the depths of the sea,[5] as that which shall never more appear or come to light, as it might at low water, if it were cast near the shore side. The iniquity of Jacob shall be sought for and not be found;[6] therefore God is said to blot out[7] the iniquities of poor penitents, as

1 2 Peter 3:15.
2 Colossians 2:14.
3 Hebrews 8:12.
4 Isaiah 38:17.
5 Micah 7:19.
6 Jeremiah 50:20.
7 Isaiah 43:25.

the memorandum of a debt is blotted out when it is paid or pardoned; he not only crosses the book, which leaves it legible, but blots it out, not to be read; for so is the promise to a true penitent, *All his transgressions that he hath committed shall not be mentioned unto him*,[1] he shall not be so much as upbraided with them. It is *blotted out as a cloud, as a thick cloud*, by the heat of the sun; it is *vanished*, and there appears not the least remainder of it. The transgression is removed from the transgressors as far as the east is from the west.[2] These and many the like expressions, give us abundant assurance that the sin once pardoned shall not rise up in judgment against the sinner another day; and give us abundant occasion to say, *Who is a God like unto thee, pardoning iniquity?*

Well, this secures the life, and happiness, and eternal welfare of the penitent believer: but still he may want present comfort. The bond may be cancelled, and he not know it; the sentence of absolution passed, and yet he not hear the voice of joy and gladness;[3] so that the broken bones are still complaining: therefore God is pleased many times to carry this act of grace on yet further.

(3.) He gives an acquittance, and delivers it by his Spirit into the believer's hand, speaking peace

---

1 Ezekiel 18:22.
2 Psalm 103:12.
3 Psalm 51:8.

to him, filling him with comfort, arising from a sense of his justification, and the blessed tokens and pledges of it. When he says, *Son, daughter, be of good cheer, thy sins are forgiven thee;*[1] (as he spoke comfortably unto Zion, saying, Thy warfare is accomplished, thine iniquity is pardoned[2]) then he gives up the bond cancelled, to the unspeakable satisfaction of the penitent. We read of a woman who had been a sinner, a notorious sinner, who, upon her repentance, had much forgiven her, and showed it by her loving much;[3] yet afterwards Christ not only said of her, *Her sins which are many are forgiven*, but turned and said to her, *Thy sins are forgiven thee*, and *Thy faith hath saved thee*, to set forth this further act of divine favor, in causing us to hear God's loving-kindness, and to taste that he is gracious.

Well, blessed, thrice blessed are they whose iniquities are thus forgiven, and to whom they are not imputed; who by their own experience of the breaking of the power of sin in them, are made to know that the guilt of sin is removed; and to whom it appears, by their being reconciled to God, and to his whole will, that God is in Christ reconciled to them. But may it be hoped that these criminals shall not only be pardoned, but preferred, and made

---

1 Matthew 9:2.

2 Isaiah 40:2.

3 Luke 7:47, 48.

favorites again? Yes, to complete the mercy, he not only forgives the debts we have contracted, but,

(4.) He condescends to deal with us again, and to admit us into covenant and communion with himself. Though we have gone behind-hand in our rent, he remits the arrears, and continues us his tenants; though we have buried and wasted our talents, yet he continues us in his service, and intrusts us with more. Those we have been great losers by, though we may forgive them, yet we do not forget them, nor care for trusting them again. But in this, as in other things, the God with whom we have to do, is *God and not man;* he *forgives* and *forgets,* and yet will be no loser in his glory by forgiving. Lord! what is man, that he should be thus regarded? that he should not only be delivered from going down to the pit, but that his life should see the light,[1] the eternal light, and the paths that lead to it. When we pray that God would forgive us our debts, we pray not only that we may not be rejected, but that we may be accepted in the Beloved, according to the riches of that grace wherein he has abounded toward us;[2] that with the remission of sins, we may receive the gift of the Holy Ghost,[3] the earnest of the Spirit, and *that,* at length, which it is the earnest of, even an inheritance among all them who are

---

1 Job 33:28.
2 Ephesians 1:6, 7.
3 Acts 2:38.

sanctified; for whom he justified them he glorified.

2. Having seen how much is included in God's forgiving us our debts, because it is so great a favor, that we may be tempted to think it too much for such worthless unworthy creatures as we are to expect, let us next inquire, *what ground we have to hope for it:* how is it that a God infinitely just and holy, should be thus readily reconciled to a guilty and polluted sinner upon his repenting? If we owe a great sum of money to a man like ourselves, we could not have the face to go to him, and desire him to remit it, when we have not wherewithal to make any composition with him. Why should not a just debt be paid? and if nothing is to be had, why should not the debtor be sold,[1] *currat lex—and the law take its course?* What reason have we to expect that the lawful captive should be delivered?[2] Blessed be God we may expect it, we may be sure of it, if we repent and believe the gospel.

(1.) We may ground our expectations upon the *goodness of his nature.* This is so much his glory, that by it he has proclaimed his name not only *gracious and merciful* in general, but in this particular instance, so that he forgives iniquity, transgression, and sin;[3] and therefore pardons the sin, because he desires not nor delights in the ruin of the sinner.

---

1 Matthew 18:25.

2 Isaiah 49:24.

3 Ezekiel 34:6, 7.

How vast were the compassions of that prince in the parable, which moved him to forgive so great a debt, as that of ten thousand talents![1] And yet, as heaven is high above the earth, so do the divine compassions exceed those: Israel of old found them so, when their transgressions were so very numerous, so very heinous; yet he being full of compassion, forgave their iniquity. Merciful men will sometimes lend, hoping for nothing again; and where nothing is to be had, will not be rigorous nor extreme in demanding their right: and shall not the Father of mercies take pity on the miserable? He who is good, and therefore ready to forgive; merciful and gracious,[2] and therefore removes our transgressions from us as far as the east is from the west.[3] He is a God with whom that plea is of force, *What profit is there in my blood?* And whose soul was grieved for the misery of Israel,[4] though they brought it upon themselves by their own sin and folly.

Well, it is true that God is infinitely good, and we have abundant reason to hope in his mercy, and abundant encouragement to plead it with him; but it is as true that he is just and righteous, that he is the great Governor of the world, and the honor of his government must be maintained; his injured

---

1 Matthew 18:27.
2 Psalm 86:5.
3 Psalm 103:8, 12.
4 Judges 10:16.

justice calls for satisfaction, and one attribute of his shall not be glorified by the damage and reproach of another. It is true, he is merciful, and yet there is a world of angels who lie, and are like to lie for ever, under the pouring out of the full vials of his wrath; and therefore, though his goodness and mercy, as it is revealed to us in the Scripture, is our great encouragement, yet,

(2.) We are to ground our expectations upon the *mediation of our Lord Jesus*. Therefore God forgives our debt, because Jesus Christ, by the blood of his cross, has made satisfaction for it, and given his life a ransom for ours: which is so far from lessening the freeness of that grace which forgives us, that it greatly magnifies it, for it was he himself who found the ransom,[1] it was he himself who gave his Son to be a propitiation for our sins.[2] And herein more than in any thing he commended his love,[3] that he would not only forgive our debt, but put himself to such vast expense of blood and treasure, that he might do it so as to secure, nay to declare, his righteousness; *to declare, I say, at this time his righteousness;* (such an emphasis does the apostle lay upon this) that he might be not only merciful but just, and the justifier of them who believe in Jesus.[4]

---

1 Job 33:24.

2 1 John 4:10.

3 Romans 5:8.

4 Romans 3:25, 26.

If sinners are debtors, it is Christ who is their surety, upon the account of whose satisfaction their debt is forgiven: Christ is called *the surety of the covenant;*[1] not that he was originally bound in the bond with us, as if it were implied in the penalty annexed to the covenant of innocency, which was, *Thou shalt surely die*, that is, *thou or thy surety*. No, Christ's undertaking supposes us already debtors, and under arrest for the debt; so that Christ comes in rather as bail to the action, than as a secondary undertaker from the beginning. His office as mediator takes it for granted, that God and man are at variance, for a *mediator is not of one;*[2] we are looked upon as under the law, that is under the curse, when Christ to redeem us makes himself sin and a curse for us.[3] Let us see how this is done.

[1.] Our Lord Jesus voluntarily undertook to be a surety for us: pitying our deplorable case, and concerned for his Father's injured honor, that divine justice might be satisfied, and yet sinners saved, he offered to make his own soul a sacrifice for sin, and himself a propitiation, answering the demands of the law, as the propitiatory, or mercy-seat, exactly answered the dimensions of the ark. The Father intrusted him with this great piece of service, and he voluntarily and cheerfully consented to it: he

---

1 Hebrews 7:22.
2 Galatians 3:20.
3 Galatians 3:10, 13.

said, *Lo, I come,* and not only did this will of God, but delighted to do it;[1] drawn to it, and held to it, with no other cords but those of his own love, and the agreeableness of his undertaking to his Father's commandment.

Christ had no debt of his own to pay, for he always did those things that pleased his Father. Such was the dignity of his person, and such the value of the price he paid, that he had wherewithal to make full satisfaction, and to pay this debt, even to the last mite. He said, *Upon me be the curse*, my Father. Thus he became bound for us, as Paul for Onesimus to Philemon his master: If *he have wronged thee, or oweth thee ought, I Paul have written it with my own hand*, the blessed Jesus has written it with his own blood, *I will repay it.*[2] And this undertaking of Christ's shall redound more to the glory of God, even to the glory of his justice, than the damnation of these sinners would have done; for if they had perished, the righteousness of God would have been, to eternity, but *in the satisfying;* but now, by the merit of Christ's death, it is once for all *satisfied,* and reconciliation made for iniquity. Thus he *restored that which he took not away.*[3]

Let us pause a little, and think with wonder and thankfulness of this glorious undertaking.

---

1 Psalm 40:7.

2 Philemon 1:18, 19.

3 Psalm 69:4.

How great was that kindness and love of God our Saviour towards man, which set this work going! How admirable the wisdom that contrived it! *The wisdom of God in a mystery*.[1] Let every crown be thrown at the Redeemer's feet, and every song sung to his praise. *Who is this that engageth his heart to approach unto God*,[2] as a surety for us? It is he who speaks in righteousness, and will never unsay what he has said, for he is mighty to save,[3] he is almighty.

[2.] Having made himself a surety for us, he made full satisfaction to divine justice for our debt, by the blood of his cross. He poured out his soul unto death,[4] not only for our good, but in our stead; and paid, though not the *idem—the same*, that we should have paid, yet the *tantundem—the equivalent*, that which was more than equivalent; so that in him God might be said to have received double for all our sins,[5] so much was the Father glorified in him.

God charged the debt upon him, according to his undertaking. Those he undertook for being insolvent, the action was brought against him; and God laid upon him the iniquity of us all;[6] made it

---

1 1 Corinthians 2:7.
2 Jeremiah 30:21.
3 Isaiah 53:1.
4 Isaiah 53:12.
5 Isaiah 40:2.
6 Isaiah 53:6.

all to *meet upon him,* (so the word is) as the sins of all Israel were made to meet upon the head of the goat, that on the day of atonement was to be sent into a land of forgetfulness.[1] Solomon says, *He that is surety for a stranger shall smart for it,* shall be broken by it: our Lord Jesus being surety for us who were strangers and foreigners, he smarted for it;[2] for it pleased the Lord to bruise him, and put him to grief.[3]

He voluntarily and freely paid the debt; his life was not forced from him, but he laid it down of himself.[4] The satisfaction was to be made *to God in his* HONOR; for in that he had been injured, and to that he had an eye, when he said, *Father, glorify thy name,*[5] take the satisfaction that is demanded. And it was to be made by *his death,* for without shedding of blood, that blood which is the life, there was no remission; and, therefore, he laid down his life with these words, *Father, into thy hands I commit my spirit;*[6] that life, that soul, which is to be given as a ransom for many, I here give to thee; I put it into thy hands, as the surety pays the debt into the hands of the creditor, the proper person to receive it.

[3.] The satisfaction which Christ made for our

---

1 Leviticus 16:21.
2 Proverbs 11:15.
3 Isaiah 53:10.
4 John 10:18.
5 John 12:28.
6 Luke 23:45.

sins was graciously accepted, and God was so well pleased in him,[1] as to be well pleased with us in him. This was a further act of divine grace: for in strict justice it might have been insisted on, that the law should have had its course against the sinners themselves. Christ intimated, that pursuant to the counsels of peace,[2] which were between the Father and him, concerning man's redemption, his arrest should be our discharge, when he said to those who seized him in the garden, *If ye seek me, let these go their way*.[3] He delivered up himself to suffer and die, that we might be delivered from wrath and ruin, and divine justice agreed to it.

In token of the acceptance of his satisfaction, God raised him from the dead, sent an angel to roll away the stone from the door of the sepulchre, and so to release the prisoner; which he did, and then sat upon it[4] in triumph, signifying that then death had no more dominion over him, but was perfectly conquered and abolished. But are we certain that he had a fair discharge? Yes, for he was often seen alive, seen at liberty, and the Father having raised him from the dead, set him at his own right hand, which would have been no place for him, if he had not fully made good his undertaking. Christ's death

---

1 Matthew 17:5.
2 Zechariah 6:13.
3 John 18:8.
4 Matthew 28:2.

being the payment of our debt, for he was delivered for our offenses, his resurrection was the taking out of our acquittance, for he rose again for our justification.[1] Therefore the apostle lays the stress of our faith, hope, and comfort upon this, *Who is he that shall condemn?* Who can take out an execution against us? *It is Christ that died, yea, rather, that is risen again:*[2] by which it appears that his dying for us was accepted, especially since he now is even at the right hand of God making intercession in the virtue of his satisfaction; and it is an effectual intercession, for the Father hears him always.

[4.] The satisfaction being accepted, a release of debts is published and proclaimed in the everlasting gospel to all penitent and obedient believers. Full assurance is given them that their sins shall be pardoned, and they shall be made accepted in the Beloved. The preaching of the gospel is called the *proclaiming of the acceptable year of the Lord,*[3] in allusion to the year of release, which was every seventh; and, especially, to the year of jubilee, which was every fiftieth;[4] when all debts were discharged, mortgaged possessions restored, and all encumbrances on men's estates taken off. And this was proclaimed by sound of trumpet in the evening

---

1 Romans 4:25.
2 Romans 8:34.
3 Luke 4:19.
4 Leviticus 25:9, 10.

of the day of atonement, to signify, that upon the account of the atonement which Christ was to make, poor sinners should be delivered from that wrath and curse to which they were bound over, and brought into the glorious liberty of God's children, and restored to all the glorious privileges and inheritances of free-born Israelites. *Blessed is the people that hear this joyful sound,*[1] the trumpet of the everlasting gospel publishing this release, this act of indemnity, *liberty to the captives, and the opening of the prison to them that were bound.*

These glad tidings of great joy are to be brought to all people; whoever will come and take the benefit of this general release, and sue out a particular discharge upon it, on very easy and unexceptionable terms; for the gospel excludes none, who do not by their own wilful impenitence and unbelief exclude themselves. Nay, we have not only this discharge offered us, but we are courted, and earnestly invited, to come in and accept of it. God having in Christ laid a foundation for the reconciling the world unto himself, has sent his ambassadors, not only to propose the matter to us, but to beseech us, nay, God does by them *beseech us to be reconciled to God,*[2] though it had better become us to beseech him first to be reconciled to us.

[5.] It is upon the account of Christ's satisfaction,

---

1 Psalm 89:15.
2 2 Corinthians 5:19, 20.

that our sins are actually pardoned upon our repenting and believing; and that is it which we are to plead with God, and to rely upon as a valid plea in our prayers to God for the forgiveness of our debts. In *his* righteousness we must appear before God; making mention of that, even of that only, and not thinking to justify ourselves.[1] It is through his blood that we have redemption, even the remission of sins,[2] for that is it which, having been shed for us without the city, speaks for us within the veil, and speaks better things than that of Abel;[3] and he still appears *in the midst of the throne*, a Lamb *as it had been slain*,[4] newly slain, and bleeding afresh, to intimate the constant perpetual virtue of his satisfaction, and the continual advantage which believers have and may have by it.

In praying for the forgiveness of our sins, we must have an eye to Christ as our Redeemer; the Redeemer of our persons that were in bondage, and of our inheritance which was in mortgage. He is our *Goel;*[5] Job calls him so, and the prophets often: it is the title of the next *kinsman;* who by the law was to redeem the possession which his brother sold.[6]

---

1 Psalm 71:16.
2 Ephesians 1:7.
3 Hebrews 12:24.
4 Revelation 5:6.
5 Goel—redeemer.
6 Leviticus 25:25.

Christ having taken our nature upon him, is become our kinsman, and he is the next kinsman who is able to redeem, so that to him the right of redemption does belong: and he has graciously condescended to do the kinsman's part; so that we return to our inheritance again, from which we had otherwise been for ever banished; and have the earnest of it until the complete redemption of the purchased possession.[1] We must also in a particular manner have an eye to his death as our ransom: for the sake of which we are delivered from going down to the pit.[2] Very fitly therefore is that sacrament which is the memorial of his death, made the seal of our pardon.

3. Having showed you how sad your case is upon the account of sin, and what a dangerous debt it is; and yet that your case is not desperate, but there is hope for you through grace, I promise myself, you will now be willing and glad to hear, *what is expected and required from you*, that you may obtain this favor, and that your debts may be forgiven. Christ, as a surety for us, has made satisfaction; but what must we do that we may have an interest in that satisfaction? It is true that atonement is made for sin, and is accepted as sufficient to ground a treaty of peace upon; and yet it is as true, that multitudes perish eternally under the load of this debt, and continue in their captivity, notwithstanding the proclamation

1 Ephesians 1:4.
2 Job 33:24.

of liberty. It therefore concerns us all to see to it, that we be duly qualified, according to the tenor of the new covenant, for the comforts of a sealed pardon and a settled peace; and that we may be so,

(1.) We must *confess the debt*, with a humble, lowly, penitent, and obedient heart. We must own ourselves guilty before God, and concluded under sin. Let not those expect to prosper, or recover themselves from under this load, who cover their sins, for they, and they only, who confess and forsake them, shall find mercy.[1] We are charged as debtors, and must not go about to deny the debt, no, nor to excuse or extenuate it; but be ready to acknowledge that we have sinned, and have perverted that which was right, and it profited us not;[2] that we have been both unjust to God and injurious to ourselves, as debtors are.

In confessing the debt we must be particular; must not only own that we are sinners, but, in *this* and *the other* instance, we have sinned; not for information to God, he knows our sins better than we ourselves know them, but for humiliation and warning to ourselves. *I have sinned*, (says David) *and have done this evil.*[3] *I have sinned*, (says Achan) *and thus and thus have I done.*[4] And the more

---

1 Proverbs 28:13.
2 Job 33:27.
3 Psalm 51:4.
4 Joshua 7:20.

particular we are in the acknowledgment of sin, the more comfort we may expect to have in the sense of the pardon. If I can say, *"This* sin I confessed; I trust, through grace, *this* sin is pardoned, and shall not be laid to my charge." But then this confession of sin must be accompanied with true remorse and godly sorrow for it: we must bewail it, and bemoan ourselves because of it; must give glory to God, and take shame to ourselves in making this confession. And as the prodigal when we own we have sinned against God, we must own, that we are no more worthy to be called his children; nay, that it were a righteous thing with him to deliver us to the tormentors. And if we thus judge ourselves, we shall not be judged.

(2.) We must *acknowledge a judgment* of all we have to our Lord Jesus, who has been thus kind to satisfy for our debt. This is one proper act of faith. To resign, surrender, and give up ourselves, our whole selves, body, soul, and spirit; all we are, have, and can do; to be under the direction and government of his word and Spirit, to be devoted to his honor, employed in his service, and disposed of at his will. Our own selves we must give unto the Lord,[1] and to us to live must be Christ: our all must be put into his hands, must be laid at his feet. It is indeed a very poor counter-security, but such as it is he requires it, and is pleased to accept of it,

1 2 Corinthians 8:5.

provided we be sincere and faithful in the surrender.

There is good reason why we should do this; for therefore he delivered us out of the hands of our enemies, that we might serve him;[1] therefore redeemed us, that we might be to him a *peculiar* people, *purified* from sinful works, and *zealous of good works*.[2] Nor can we do better for ourselves, than to give up ourselves entirely to Christ; we are never *more our own*, than when we are *wholly his*. If we resign ourselves to him, it is in trust for the securing of ourselves, and our own true welfare, that we may not again be our own ruin. Thus will he complete his kindness to us, if it be not our own fault: he who was our surety to save us from perishing under the load of guilt we had contracted, will be our trustee, to save us from falling again under the like load; for he has said, *Sin shall not have dominion over you*.[3] Thus will he perfect all that which concerns us;[4] and if we commit ourselves and our all to him, we shall find he is able to keep what we have committed unto him against that day, and he will be found a faithful trustee.

(3.) We must *give to Christ the honor* of our pardon, by relying entirely on his righteousness as our plea for it; acknowledging that other foundation of

---

1 Luke 1:74, 75.

2 Titus 2:14.

3 Psalm 138:8.

4 2 Timothy 1:12.

hope can no man lay,[1] and other fountain of joy can no man open. We must for ever disclaim all dependence upon our own sufficiency, and with the highest satisfaction rest upon Christ only as a complete and all-sufficient Saviour. The great concerns of our immortal souls, our reconciliation to God, and our felicity in him, we most lodge in his hands, by a submission not only to his government, as the *Lord our Ruler*, but to his grace, as *the Lord our Righteousness*, made of God to us *righteousness*,[2] that we might be *made the righteousness of God in him*.[3] For, thus, boasting is for ever excluded, and he that glories must glory in the Lord.

(4.) We must *study what we shall render to him who has loved us, who has so loved us*. Let us mention it to his praise, take all occasions to speak of that great love wherewith he loved us, in purchasing for us the remission of that great debt. We cannot expect an interest in Christ and his righteousness, unless we be willing to own our obligations to him, as those who are sensible the bonds he has loosed us from[4] bind us closely and constantly to him.

(5.) We must *engage ourselves for the future*, that we will render to God the things that are his, and be careful not to run in debt again. If we would

---

1 1 Corinthians 3:11.
2 1 Corinthians 1:30.
3 2 Corinthians 5:21.
4 Psalm 116:16.

find mercy, we must not only confess our sins, but forsake them, and keep close to the way of our duty. Ceasing to do evil, and learning to do well, are the commanded fruits of repentance, and without those we cannot expect the promised fruits of it. Has God graciously remitted us our arrears, let us pay our rent more punctually for time to come. Every day is a rent day with us, and we must be careful, by filling up time with duty, and doing the work of every day in its day, to pay our rent duly; and wherein we come short, balance our accounts with the blood of Christ, which cleanses from all sin,[1] by a renewed application of the virtue of that to our souls; and thus *keep touch* with him who is, and ever will be, faithful to us. Have we wasted our talents,[2] and so contracted debt, and yet are we still intrusted with them? Let us henceforth be more diligent in the improvement of them, that by the blessing and grace of our Master, our five talents may be made other five, and we may have our Master's approbation, and enter at length into his joy. And let us always remember, that God speaks peace to his people, and to his saints, on this condition, that they do not return again to folly.[3]

(6.) Our forgiving others is made the indispensable condition of our being forgiven of God.

---

1 1 John 1:7.

2 Matthew 25:20.

3 Psalm 85:8.

Nothing can be more express than this, *If we forgive not men their trespasses, neither will our Father who is in heaven forgive us ours.*[1] For God will have his children to be like him, merciful as he is merciful, and good as he is, even to the evil and unthankful. That servant in the parable, who was rigorous in exacting a small debt from his fellow-servant, by that instance of the hardness of his heart made it to appear, that he was never truly humbled for his own debt to his Lord, that great debt, nor ever truly sensible of his Lord's kindness to him in forgiving it; and therefore, his repentance being counterfeit, his pardon was never ratified, but he was delivered to the tormentors, as a wicked servant.[2]

Let this consideration prevail to pacify the most provoked, and mollify the most severe; let it not only suppress every root of bitterness in us, but extirpate it and pluck it up: let us not harbor the least thoughts of malice and revenge against those who have been any way injurious to us, nor render to any evil for evil, nor be extreme to mark what is done amiss against us; for *what then shall we do, when God riseth up, and when he visiteth, what shall we answer him?*[3]

And now, (brethren) having very briefly and plainly opened to you this great concern that lies

---

1 Matthew 6:14, 15.
2 Matthew 18:32, 34.
3 Job 31:14.

between you and God, I must leave it to you to make the application of what has been said, each of you to yourselves; nay, I hope you have been applying it as we have gone along; for these are things of which none of us can say, They belong not to us. Leave it to you, did I say?—I leave it with God by his Spirit to apply it to all your consciences, that you may be *delivered into the mold* of these great truths. I shall therefore close only with a few words of exhortation upon the whole matter.

1. Do not delay to come to an account with your own consciences, but search diligently and impartially, that you may see how matters stand between you and God. *Consider your ways,*[1] *search and try them.*[2] Commune with your own hearts, saying. *What have I done?* What have I done amiss? Take an account of your debts to God, as all prudent tradesmen do of their debts to those with whom they deal. Think how many the particulars are, how great the sum total is, and what circumstances have enhanced the debt, and run it up to a great height; how exceeding sinful your sins have been, how exceeding hateful to God, and hurtful to yourselves. Put that question to yourselves which the unjust steward put to his lord's debtors, *How much owest thou unto my Lord?* and tell the truth as they did, for themselves; and do not think to impose upon

1 Haggai 1:5.
2 Lamentations 3:40.

God, by making the matter better than it is, as the steward did for them, writing fifty for a hundred.[1]

2. Be thoroughly convinced of your misery and danger by reason of sin; see process ready to be taken out against you, and consider what is to be done: it is no time to trifle, when all you have is ready to be seized, and if the present season be slipped, you know not how soon the things that belong to your peace may be for ever hid from your eyes, and you will rue your carelessness when it is too late to retrieve what you have lost by it.

3. Agree with your adversary quickly, while you are in the way with him;[2] make your peace with God, and do it with all speed. You need not *send to desire conditions of peace*,[3] they are offered to you, if you will but accept of them; and they are not only easy but very advantageous. Take the advice which Solomon gives to his son who is ensnared in suretyship. *Do this, my son*, that thou mayest deliver thyself, go humble thyself, and thereby thou wilt not only pacify an adversary, but make sure a friend: and give not sleep to thine eyes, nor slumber to thine eyelids, till thou hast done this.[4]

4. In order to the making of your peace with God, make sure your interest in Jesus Christ, and

---

1 Luke 16:5, 6.
2 Matthew 5:25.
3 Luke 14:32.
4 Proverbs 6:3, 4.

make use of him daily for that purpose: retain him of counsel for you in this great cause on which your all depends, and let him be not only your plea but your pleader, for that is his office; *If any man sin, and so run into debt, we have an advocate with the Father*,[1] who is ready to appear for us, and attends continually to this very thing. Be advised by him, as the client is by his counsel, and then refer yourselves to him, put your case into his hand and say, *Thou shall answer, Lord, for me*, when I have nothing to say for myself.

5. Renew your repentance every day for your sins of daily infirmity, and be earnest with God in prayer for the pardon of them. Hereby we give to God the glory of his never-failing mercy, which abundantly pardons; and to Christ the glory of his inexhaustible merit and grace; and keep ourselves continually easy by leaving no guilt to lie upon the conscience unrepented of. "Even reckonings (we say) make long friends." And the more we are humbled for our daily sins, and the more we see of our obligation to Christ, and his merit, for the pardon of them, the more watchful we shall be against them, and the more careful to abstain from all appearances of evil, and approaches towards it.

Lastly, Let those to whom much is forgiven, love much.[2] We have all of us much forgiven us, it

---

1 1 John 2:1.
2 Luke 7:42, 43.

is a very *great debt* from which we have been discharged: now it may be expected, that we should have only hearts accordingly enlarged in gratitude to him who *first* loved us, who *so* loved us, and gave himself for us, loved us and washed us from our sins in his own blood. How shall we express our love to him? What box of precious ointment shall we pour upon his head? What song of love shall we sing to his praise! O that the love of Christ may constrain us[1] to love him, and live to him, who loved us and died for us; to be faithful and constant in our love to him, who having loved his own which were in the world, loveth them unto the end,[2] and will love them all at length into the world of everlasting love.

---

1 2 Corinthians 5:14.
2 John 13:1.

NOTES

NOTES

MAN'S QUESTIONS & GOD'S ANSWERS

Am I accountable to God?
Each of us will give an account of himself to God. Romans 14:12 (NIV).

Has God seen all my ways?
Everything is uncovered and laid bare before the eyes of him to whom we must give account. Hebrews 4:13 (NIV).

Does he charge me with sin?
But the Scripture declares that the whole world is a prisoner of sin. Galatians 3:22 (NIV).
All have sinned and fall short of the glory of God. Romans 3:23 (NIV).

Will he punish sin?
The soul who sins is the one who will die. Ezekiel 18:4 (NIV).
For the wages of sin is death, but the gift of God is eternal life in Christ Jesus our Lord. Romans 6:23 (NIV).

Must I perish?
He is patient with you, not wanting anyone to perish, but everyone to come to repentance. 2 Peter 3:9 (NIV).

How can I escape?
Believe in the Lord Jesus, and you will be saved. Acts 16:31 (NIV).

Is he able to save me?
Therefore he is able to save completely those who come to God through him. Hebrews 7:25 (NIV).

Is he willing?
Christ Jesus came into the world to save sinners. 1 Timothy 1:15 (NIV).

Am I saved on believing?
Whoever believes in the Son has eternal life, but whoever rejects the Son will not see life, for God's wrath remains on him. John 3:36 (NIV).

Can I be saved now?
Now is the time of God's favor, now is the day of salvation. 2 Corinthians 6:2 (NIV).

As I am?
Whoever comes to me I will never drive away. John 6:37 (NIV).

Shall I not fall away?
Him who is able to keep you from falling. Jude 1:24 (NIV).

If saved, how should I live?
Those who live should no longer live for themselves but for him who died for them and was raised again. 2 Corinthians 5:15 (NIV).

What about death and eternity?
I am going there to prepare a place for you. I will come back and take you to be with me that you also may be where I am. John 14:2-3 (NIV).